SUBWOOFER

New Issues Poetry & Prose

Editor	William Olsen
Guest Editor	Nancy Eimers
Managing Editor	Kimberly Kolbe
Layout Editor	Sarah Kidd
Assistant Editor	Ephraim Sommers

New Issues Poetry & Prose
The College of Arts and Sciences
Western Michigan University
Kalamazoo, MI 49008

First Edition, 2017.

ISBN-13   978-1-936970-50-6 (paperbound)

Library of Congress Cataloging-in-Publication Data:
Rothman, Wesley.
SUBWOOFER/Wesley Rothman
Library of Congress Control Number   2016919573

Art Director	Nicholas Kuder
Designer	Diana Giacobone
Production Manager	Paul Sizer
	The Design Center, Frostic School of Art
	College of Fine Arts
	Western Michigan University
Printing	McNaughton & Gunn, Inc.

SUBWOOFER

Wesley Rothman

New Issues Press

WESTERN MICHIGAN UNIVERSITY

for Megan

for our lowest frequencies

Contents

●

Request Aubade 11

The Invention of Clock Theory 12

Request Hour 13

Rum & Raspberries 14

Epistle 15

Throbbing in the Bush 16

Portrait of Subwoofer as Holiest Holy 17

The Republic of Beat 18

I Pledge 20

Sinnerman 21

Esther 23

Ruins 24

The Sleepers 25

Exodus 28

To Do This 29

●

Oyster Elegy 33

) swallow (35

Song, Remembered 37

Bars of Blue 38

SAMO© Blues 40

Baptism 42

Threnody: Your Boom & Treble Silence 44

Whiteness As Hyperbolic Bass Line 45

The Salt Craving 46

Litany of Hustle 47

The Emperor of White Smoke 48

Whiteness 49

•

This Time, Fire   55
What Is Given, What Is Done   61
If Smoke Could Sing   63
How to Flip the Beat   64
If *Riot* Means Destruction   66
Uprising   67
Disturbance   68
Bass Tone Ode   69
Transubstantiation   70
Another Sip   71
Night Interrogates the Light Bulb   72
Exodus, Still   73
Plea   75
Kneebone in the Wilderness   76

Acknowledgments

About Place: "What Is Given, What Is Done"

Booth: "Request Hour"

Copper Nickel: "Whiteness"

The Cortland Review: "The Republic of Beat"

Crab Orchard Review: "Oyster Elegy," "Threnody: Your Boom & Treble Silence" (as "Your Boom & Treble Silence")

Crazyhorse: "Plea"

Day One: "Exodus"

Gulf Coast: "Bars of Blue"

Harvard Review: "Rum & Raspberries"

The Los Angeles Review: "Litany of Hustle," "Transubstantiation"

Mississippi Review: "Kneebone in the Wilderness"

Narrative Magazine: "Disturbance"

New England Review: "Throbbing in the Bush," "I Pledge" (as "Pledge")

The New Guard: "To Do This"

Poet Lore: "Portrait of Subwoofer as Holiest Holy"

Poetry Northwest: "The Sleepers"

Post Road: "Sinnerman"

Prairie Schooner: "The Salt Craving," "If Smoke Could Sing"

Solstice: "Ruins" (as "The Ruins")

Southern Humanities Review: "Another Sip"

Southern Indiana Review: "Baptism"

Sporklet: "Night Interrogates the Light Bulb"

Third Coast: "Bass Tone Ode"

Vinyl Poetry: "SAMO© Blues," "The Invention of Clock Theory"

Waccamaw: "Whiteness As Hyperbolic Bass Line" (as "Hyperbolic Bass Line")

Waxwing: "How to Flip the Beat"

"Throbbing in the Bush" appears in the *Poets on Growth Anthology* (Math Paper Press).

"The Invention of Clock Theory" and "Ruins" appear in *The Best Emerging Poets of 2014 Anthology* (Stay Thirsty Media).

"If Riot Means Destruction" appears in *The Outrage Project; Split This Rock's Poems That Resist Police Brutality & Demand Racial Justice*; and the *Philadelphia Review of Books* blog.

SUBWOOFER is the result of history & influence. The immense gratitude I have for those who have given their love & challenge is not enough; they deserve all praise & love. To my gracious mentors & teachers, Jericho Brown, Eduardo C. Corral, Rick Barot, Carlton Floyd, John Skoyles, Gail Mazur, Pablo Medina, Susan Tomlinson, Jonathan Aaron, Irene Williams, Peter Jay Shippy, Margo Wilding, Kevin Timpe, Michael Wiegers, thank you, in every way possible.

To friends, tireless supporters, & those who have made their mark from a distance, Douglas Kearney, Phillip B. Williams, Leah Umansky, Metta Sáma, Ailish Hopper, Sean Hill, James Allen Hall, Kevin Simmonds, Sarah Browning, C. Dale Young, January Gill O'Neil, Jenny Barber, Marcus Wicker, Martha Collins, Natalie Diaz, Don Share, Rachel Eliza Griffiths, Ladan Osman, Oliver de la Paz, Jon Tribble, Allison Joseph, David Tomas Martinez, Wayne Miller, Richard Siken, Mark Bibbins, Jennifer Jean, Krysten Hill, Rosebud Ben-Oni, Joseph Legaspi, Danielle Jones-Pruett, Daniel Pritchard, Rigoberto González, Cyrus Cassells, Cathy Park Hong, Phillip Lopate, Natalie Earnhart, coconspirators at Mass Poetry, *Ploughshares*, Copper Canyon Press, *Salamander*, Emerson College, Berklee College of Music, Suffolk University, UMass Boston, the University of San Diego, & the Vermont Studio Center, thank you for your selflessness & kindness.

For your remarkable support, thank you Shane McCrae, Yona Harvey, Major Jackson, Adrian Matejka & Mary Szybist.

Thank you for your unending patience, support, & expertise Kim Kolbe, Sarah Kidd, Nancy Eimers, Bill Olsen, Paul Sizer, & everyone else at New Issues & Western Michigan University who made this book live.

To so many students who have challenged, encouraged, dared, & revitalized me & these poems, thank you.

The on-living spirits of Nina Simone, James Baldwin, Audre Lorde, Ralph Ellison, Gwendolyn Brooks, Gloria Anzaldúa, Lucille Clifton, Adrienne Rich, Jake Adam York, Amiri Baraka, & a litany of living poets, writers, & artists are the foundation of this book, the guides to whom I am ever indebted.

& my permanent gratitude & love to my family: my parents—Pam & Robin, the Menconis, L.L., & the one who keeps me most grounded & moving in this life, Megan. My gratitude doesn't begin to cover what you have done for me & these pages.

●

Who knows, but that, on the lower frequencies I speak...

—Ralph Ellison, *Invisible Man*

*The record is there for all to read. It resounds all over the world.
It might as well be written in the sky.*

—James Baldwin, "The White Man's Guilt"

Request Aubade

Why shouldn't doves suddenly still
In their sky every time a last breath flies?

Maybe they do. Maybe we lock up too,
Stricken oblivious. If the meat of clouds

Freeze-frames, if our eyes remain wide
A hair longer than usual, if we're stuck

For the moment each human leaves their humanness
Behind, I want to know it. To acknowledge

That fraction of time the way I do a fawn in the yard
Nabbing cherries from the low branches with its tongue,
The way I hold whomever will hold me near the end

Of the most crushing, bloodiest days. Let me breathe
That loss. Let its ripening seep from my lungs.

Let us pause in our busy-making,
Make the pause busy with breaking—

A slender-stemmed wine glass
Tipping in the center, for the hot breeze of grief.

Let us shatter & in our repair never be completely
Crackless. Let us—whoever you are, there, listening.

The Invention of Clock Theory

A child is born with no state of mind.
I was born with a blank tongue,
Blind to the ways of mankind,

Running fresh as a new clock's grind.
Ticker talking strong, with tip top lungs
A child is born. With no state of mind

I grew in my white, such a tight clock-wind.
Howled & whooped through youth, strung
Blind. To the ways of mankind

I wound myself locked, bolted in design
Til another take took a question, stung.
A child is born with new state of mind

When a step falls out of time, behind
Or off-beat in clock speak, flung
From blind ways of a white man's kind.

A clock's arms run round its heart, so fine.
I *lived so fast & died so young,* young one.
A child is born with no state of mind, blind
To the ways of humankind, of beats & binds.

Request Hour

feat. DJ Mirror

Give me a set list of wrecking ball bass, boxer fists laced,

Give me jackhammer & TNT. Give me a bullet screaming

At itself to halt, backtrack, re-jacket, melt down. Give me

The self, deconstructed, its blueprints in sound waves.

Break it down with liner notes, then cut-up, mix & remix

& remix the remix. Give me beats larger than longing—

Wider, longer, deeper. There, in your reflecting glass,

Spin a track with my sweat & desperate prayers. Etch me

Into vinyl, then defile the groove. Now is the hour

My tearing down—the record written in the sky—

Finally topples me. This tune must become an anthem,

Must whir & thunder as blood still cooped, manifesting.

Amplify the lowest lowdown notes, nos, & nonsense

I've thumped, the loudmouth breakings I've trumped,

The hardest bass lines I've missed. Soundproof me,

Deposit every sound there is, in me. All my prayers

Are tucked in my dancing shoes. Leave me to reckon

The base of faith. Fashion me an ear-shaped heart,

A playback button & a mixtape. Please, give me something

Worth giving. Where to? If you hold the mic, who holds you?

Rum & Raspberries

The center of our galaxy tastes like raspberries
& smells of rum. We don't yet know
The center's sound. Maybe absence—
The most perfect vacuum cancelling pitch
& tenor—but I can't help hear the dits & pings
Of history waving through uninterrupted space,
Sonaring projectiles, junk, gamma rays & radio waves
Wiggling into what we name *infinity*. We, our own
Center, square off with this other center, the roar & thrum
Solar flares shrug, strumming the long, thick string
Of the galaxy. We make our noise insistently. I can't help
But hear transmissions fading from their unidentified
Sources, hear the plump tartness of raspberries,
Their cocoon of subwoofers, a spiral of seeds
Suspended in ruby belief. The galaxy center clinks,
Ice melting in a rocked rum. Ice sends the sound
Swimming around & round & bouncing. The trick
Is to finish the drink quickly enough without tilting
The axis of this monstrous rotation, this breaking order.
Or isn't that why we believe in brown liquor, to knock
Things off-center a bit, for a time? The drink thumps
Down my throat, the locus of vibration & sound,
Where I find a chamber in which I'm intimate
With my ignorance. I pour another so the buzz
Keeps zipping out there & in here.

Epistle

You are here because
a million people holler.
    —Douglas Kearney

Listen to the sirens, their clockwork
Of question. Listen for the quiet lie,
Nudging you nearer the far side
Of the mind, leading. Listen
To the silence you do not interrupt.
Listen to choices, the words
You yoke around every stranger. Listen
& hear shaken voices,
Breath hot on your face.
Hear the body, tongue that it is.
Listen to the city's syncopated pulse,
Its ever-shifting beat, its tender chaos.
Listen, because every sentence is a meal
Of language, & you've never been so starved.
Everything expelled is noise, everything.
Listen to your pores oozing music. Listen
To your lover's holler, hot in ricochet,
To the low moan & silence. Listen,
Always, to silence. Listen
To the broken relay & repeat of news.
Listen to eulogy pauses, to strangers' conversations,
To the missing beats of a day. Listen, when you've heard
Too much. Your hunger for sound
Is greater than you know. & when you're filled
Speak it all in a song, at once, to fill again.

Throbbing in the Bush

Like the sacred, round surround
Of a speaker—the padded ring
That holds sound in its place—
The bush of Moses throbbed with deep
Holy. I'm no deliverer, but I know

Holy when I hear it. I see the bump
Of a sound cone & place my faith
In the source. Some divinity
Speaks. Why the bush did not char
Is why the beat does not break

Or take a break from us. It's more
Merciless than the metronome
Hanging on the wall, keeping time
For days & disasters. Where flame
Sparked in the bush, is where the pump

Of sound jumps into bone. The heat
Of plump notes does not burn
Up the vessel. I throb with hot light.
Do not come any closer. This is holy
Sound. Who am I to hear, be heard?

Portrait of Subwoofer as Holiest Holy

Ear-shaped, it scoops your every swear, your prayers,
Their private blooming, collects one-ended chats,

The questions you have for the wind, strangers, your god.
It listens flawlessly. Every word wanders in—

Into the megaphone cone, like runoff into the open earth,
Bullets into breast, a tongue reaching for another.

The ear & the mouth open round. A wider reach
Welcomes subtler sounds, crisper hisses, spreads

Frequencies farther, longer, greater timbre. Woofer hears
More than any dangling crucifix, the tucked relic,

Any small holy. & it speaks back—handmade thunder—
Speaks you soothed, rattles your slivered reflection

In the rearview. It tells you repeatedly you must succumb
To whatever runs you down—

That small holy nook you've barred from every voice.

The Republic of Beat

Here, a pledge to control, surrender
                          to another's order. Notes
Command legions of players, their made-up general. Then,
                                  the quick roll
& pause of timpani. Sense bent by sound, hollers out of line.
Drum flurries & tone
                 conduct a lightning—unwieldy lethal jitter—
Into harnesses & hardness. & cacophony exceeds its maximum mass
Stability
      until the roundness of sound rolls even its conductor
                                to submission.
The jumped-up master eyes his maker—
                  black iris of boomtown—hushes
His woofing & joins the ranks of beat-shakers. Shaking
             down the orchestra pit, the bandstand,
The car frame, throbbing
          a round gut in time. Beat weaves the air thick
    With rumble, softens the cymbal-shatter, often tames
A cornet's shrill. & outside the concert hall
               foot traffic trembles the streets.
Guttural engine sputter shudders every avenue,
                passing riverside cafés,
The cadence of teaspoons & chatter. The beat's citizenry salutes
The current whir humming the surface
          of those dusky rivers, zipping
Through the bridge mouths, through open strides
            of the unsuspecting.
     Citizens often forget their country.
            So beneath throats, bass waits
For bloomtime, where words wriggle deep & unborn.
            Under sound, the imperial

Hand, façade of fair, the lowest frequencies stir us. We fall shy of perfection
Eternally, trying to match the beat beyond our bodies—

  The ancient river flow, language's elusive pulse. & our faith
In rhythm vibrates to a hush.

                    Even when vibrations go missing,
There is vibration. Even when the foot stops tapping.

I Pledge

disobedience to the united
String of beats, to rhythm, its immortality.

To the ancient metronome of day
& night, a swift pace always

Tripping us over our own feet, our mouths
Hungry for the fat fruit of tomorrow,

A fuller, deeper timbre than today's
Tuning fork ring. To routine's

Dependable bass line. To wars,
Their drumtap volleys, blood

Beating with the swing of a body's
Throb. Obedience, less

Choice than its absence. How natural
To ease into synchronicity, fall

In line with the hefty sway & step,
A march in silence, battalions

Of mind & word cadence
& mortality, relentless & bound

To the future we can never know
As we are, but must come to—

The eventual shredding of atoms
& lifelessness for hum—

A heaven vernacular.

Sinnerman

On a good day, I can hoof a mile
In the time Ms. Simone runs down a sinner.

Down to the dark tides
Of deep notes, she calls up

Cacophony, stuns
Her suspect, the totaled conscience

Wrapped around a tree, that tree
Branching veins of memory adorned

With magnolia & too many halted
Futures stolen by the sinner,

Plucked like gleaming rubies. Running
From the siren of her voice, back pocket

Bulging with red, easy riches,
The sinner destroys choices

In the street, & I'm praying at the fat base
Of the memory tree, rapt

By prayer, my desperate whisper.
No whisper, no faith will fell the tree

So I run. If I can run the rock right up
& over the hill I can keep on running,

Running down another possible me, chasing
The me that knows a thing or three

About breaking less of the world.
But the rock runs me back

To this busted belief: I come
From where I come from

Not anywhere else. This is how I keep
Facing the melody, bent around a tree

That only the jaws of death can wrench
Away from me. & I run to the river

Pockets full of rocks. In the current
I beg the rocks *Hold me*

Still. Still the whispers, still
Roaring water, the piano crashing,

Sirens in my ear's cathedral. The power
Of doubt & glory of sound run me down

As I run, run, run, run. They prop up a dark kingdom
Where I am the feebling king & the jester, twisted.

I, the preacher searching, & the rundown sinner.

Esther

Her door remained sealed
Except for the low light line
At its crease. For years,
Each morning she muttered
From five to six. How she prepared
The day like a potter. Her hands
Walked the beads, repeating
Her prayer, her intentions. I don't know
What she felt for, if she knelt
Or laid on her side. Probably for Phil
After he died, & probably on both knees,
As you might expect. She never spoke
About them, about that hour. The last time
I saw her she was grinning & speaking
In tongues, about her life, I think. I don't know
If that was torment or ecstasy
Delivered by whoever might have been listening.

Ruins

No thing erases. No matter its might,
Myth cannot blot out the name
Sunken in alabaster. Atlantis sank
Into history's tongue. Every time
I crank open my mouth, ruins
Bare their wear & resilience. Stone faces
Corrupted by vines, blurred by haze,
Hustle their prayers jungle-wise.
There, a lost civilization wanders,
Sculpting temples & empires with blood
Duped from believers. Time looms
Hefty & desperate. There, golden idols
Pulse sunglow for the completion of stone
Upon stone upon the flesh. & the shimmer
Of gold-meal curtains sewn by loyal fingers
Parts for the emperor headed for sacrifice.
Ruler of remnants, when my mouth rolls wide,
You growl from the temple's zenith, singular eclipse,
Boom a bone-stuttering tenor across continents,
You, now, must ruin, become eternal whisper.

The Sleepers

Forbidden combinations of syllables

Hijack the mouth   the throat   shoulders

The delegating mind   If the word is taboo

Understood or otherwise   a body says it

Most abundantly   I did not know

The anatomy of it   It was my anatomy

Its throat & throttle   spit & ignorance

All sleeping in my skin   Children have a knack

For viciousness   even old children

We were 16   maybe I was 17   We howled

Until our lungs collapsed   We tired

Lobbing the word like a football

With no referee   no knowing

We were rigging the game   Which is absurd

To keep up with that metaphor   life

A game   We snarled & huffed & barked

& growled & cackled our language test   We

Absorb words   follow some leads as we

Learn to interpret this world   They are given

We accept them   We assign them

In the mind   So the seeing matches

A word gifted to us   & the word

Offered teaches us what we see

See   think   word   think   see   We saw

The word we touted across the house

Pummeling each other into the couch

We saw the word in the spit flying

We were grateful   unbridled   no one

Victim of the word was around   No

One we saw   & so thought   & so

Worded as victim   anyway   The word

Woke us into sleep   Further into sleep

The word was a sleeping pill   a trigger

Of blanks   What we saw   & so thought   & so

I am now wording as blanks   Repeated   though

It was a series of rogue shots into the night

That would peak & scream back

Into someone's living room   someone's

Unsuspecting shoulder   The word would wound

Would maim   assassinate while we slept

From birth we were groomed for this

Undercover objective   No one knew

They were training us   There never was

A coded cue   They did not want us awake

They wanted us awake in our sleep   wanted

A spot on our lungs   souring the air

That makes the word into a body of force

A war we worded   & so thought   & saw

Phantom & bodily   revised though printed

In the book of everlasting

Exodus

For a time, I am sky, lodged
Between black rock & the Colorado's
Muddy emerald murk. The splash & vertigo
Remind me that every time I smash something,
I spin out. So I flail for the surface, spasm
So I'll jolt into control. Then the air gulp
& endorphins. I paddle to the shallows,
Lift from the jetty, flutter twenty feet back up
The river's rock edge. I do it again. & again.
I launch myself into the river for hours
& the sun's fingers lancing the water above
Pull me up each time. In the early afternoon
Hawks stitch themselves across the light,
Hail the ritual of sacrificing my body
To the current, each resurrection that follows.
Every splash brief, like the tail-kick
Of a fish once it's fed, returning to a quiet depth.
But I am commanding my life to the river,
Lingering deeper each leap, before buoying
& repeating. I condemn myself to the numbing flow,
Its hazy tint, because I think I will escape it.
On these rocks I am power & am powerless
Against myself. Every time, I bust the water wide
& it grips me, asks me to stay. Then, eventually, I rise,
Dripping what I have broken, walk away from myself.

To Do This

I'll need all the history I think I own. Plus, a drum of gasoline,
Every question mark I can muster, more, more. Two megaphones—
Amplifying & listening—whatever holy text I keep in the bedside table.
I'll need one dry, strike-anywhere match, & a place to kneel.

This is key: redact comfort from my list of possessions. Once I begin,
Words will slip my mouth's grip. I will know what & how quickly to burn,
Maybe. I'll hear what I've never been able to, though the sounds haven't changed.
What I recall will grow & scorch, a pile of pallets & tires & flesh & pleasantness.

I must blaze my wheeling, smoke my wooden self. Here, here is renewal
By flame, the cleanest doubt & dose for affliction. My memories shift,
Teeth coming up & questions curling all together into the sky, so many

Black questions rising toward the blank yonder. They become a pillar
Of smoke, a sign I have begun to burn. Now, I must follow.

●

i cut a hole in his heart
nail a dozen metronomes,
each timed to the rhythm
of a newfound sinner's sigh.

—Tyehimba Jess, "fannin street signifies"

Sinner, what you gonna do
When de World's on fi-er?

—Spiritual, "What You Gonna Do?"

Oyster Elegy

I shucked dozens of oysters
      The day I learned to shuck.

      As one palm, engineered
For the contour of an oyster,

Clutched so firmly
      Its circumference, the other wedged

      Delicately. The blade split
Its meat & a finger's.

When shimmying wider
      The gap, I thought *divorce,*

      Forcibly separating one
Half from its other,

Slicing some lifeline
      Of flesh or cartilage

      From the hull. Embarking
From the familiar

Delivers a miniature death—
      Large hands tombing the lost sparrow.

      The oyster's severance: eviction & exile
To gnashing teeth,

A cave & constant tunnel.
      Such turbulent seas

Mashing, crushing
Discarded shells, fragments,

Stones ground to grain
            Found pearling, locked

            In a chamber of muscle.
Split, you ingest the meat,

Digest the past, then grief.
            An oyster opens wide

            Its mouth, offering
You the tongue.

) swallow (

All we white boys get into white vans

With coolers of white-bread peanut butter
& jelly sandwiches, crust-cut,

) swallow (

& white potato chips, with white towels
Headed for the white sand beach.

Sprinting into surf, hands slide my shins,

Browning foam, & I don't know
How to duck the curl

) swallow (

& breach,

Cleanly, the other side of a riptide. I bite
The wave as it hammers me—over-eager

Amateur rushing the ring

& some welterweight world champ.
By the time I find my feet, find the meat

Of shallows, another wave, with its question
Mark, beats me back on my ass. Set of surge

After surge, after set of surges, the hammerman,

) swallow (

Automaton of automatics drives me,
My scrawny pylon, into place, my head

Sagging at its edges & hardest at the center.
This is my known, static post of oblivion.

) swallow (

In statu quo: oblivious. No more. No glide.

No dodge. *Who controls whom? What master*
Matters the mind? How to re-member, resurrect

A mind for common good? Is re-construction
Possible for something never fully constructed?

How to salvage the full force of history, uncorrupted

& human? How to unmake

) swallow (

Me?
I wrap myself, now, with questions,

Savor the grit of sand between my teeth, the salt
Water gulp & waves' generous fury.

) swallow (

About time he drown, start again, other—

Song, Remembered

& a fire rings its fury into the person—

Bruise borne as ripple, pronounced & fading. As echo
Of the strike, pressure-turned-puncture. This, the recording—
Blues solo faded in yellow smoke. There is the slick
Rupture of *epidermis* (some steps removed from *skin*
Which belongs to a person, the wince & burn
That is theirs), pluming arteries' rush & song.
Lacerate, exacerbate the vessels, their clots;
Make them sing & sing hoarse, hold the scratch long. Then
The running whip stitch. Lasso every wound.
Soothe swelling for the mending itch. Spread balm
& ointment & antiseptic. Keep it fading,
Honest. Keep it moving, sewn, indefinitely,
To its perpetrator, the body's beaten refrain.

Bars of Blue

Hand-me-down blue, that's
our royal high-ness. This, our

glory sky—passed along, crisp as a bill,
for the end of days. Vigilante

at night. All blues bent & bending
blue booze & blue yous. Get down

debatable on this fly-highing
slinky, how to loosen the sound

of insanity: repetition, repetition, repetition, expecting the unexpected. Of course,
we'll get something fresh. This city & the next fall under different stars,

sapphire & steel, cobalt, federal. Pluck a string, plunge a piston, strike those hungry
length of your spine. What kind of blue are you-you? Snow blue, drum blue,

before-blues rubs off on you. Even when you can't hear them, they're playing you like
the same-same tune. From a different key, it's still the same old slinky-slanky tune

our kind of blue—sailed, revolutioned, majestied—hand-me-down majesty,
hot-stepping constellation of ringed colonies, rows & rows in an old

true-skewed blue. Prayer vigil for the slaughtered. Everyday vigil
vigil. Vigilance for the unknown hour when justice floats. People blues

a body abed. The locomotion of a blue train chugging blue smoke &
hearted, bend your heart low to learn how inescapable blue is, un-

album known as America, the bluetiful. Because the west end taught me
of *languorous* & *lackadaisical.* Bruisy music strikes up the fat sobs of futility, the verdict

when we play this same tune in the next city, or the city after,
towns of different stripes, crowds indigo & midnight,

wooden notes. How they grumble the whole upright the whole
brushed high-hat-in-a-club-forty-years-back blue? That

yellowed sheet music, fingers worn narrow chiming the same tune,
the sweet land of bright blue spangles, gleaming cities covered in you.

SAMO© Blues

Same old verdict
Same ol' war tug
Same old same old

Same old sucker punch
SAMO© hoodie
Same name shame

Same, oh it's the same
Same excuse & abuse
Same

Same ol' fire tearing up
Same old fire eye, fire fist
Some old world shit

Same back & forth spitting
Same old blowtorching
The human code

Same old same old same
O, same old broke down
Minds, busted hearts

Bloodied on the sidewalk
Jumped by history's street
Corner knowledge

Corner pocket of a cotton
Mogul's suit, pocket square
Turning out centuries

Of major & minorities
Beneath fractions
The dirty hive mind hum

Some SAMO© for your coffee
Same-o in your sweet tea
Same old shit for the same old fee

Same ol' scratched record
Hopping grooves in the statehouse
Same old volley across the aisle

Same old division within parties
In movements in ideologies
Same old SAMO©

SAMO© IS DEAD
SAMO© is risen SAMO©
~~Will come again~~ lives on

Baptism

A mother prone on the altar of asphalt
Where her son was run down & out
Of this world, the petals of her bouquet
Soak in ghost blood, the remnant
Since disposed, the body hoisted
Into an off-duty's truck. Crime shows

Lead us to believe a medical examiner
Will appear, give the body its nearly final
Tenderness, that someone will usher
The boy beyond. The crime shows
Lead us to believe in justice
& funerals, that night might be safe, hell,

That day might be safe, warm in summer's
Long dusk, that afternoons are meant
For sweet tea down the throat, children through
The sprinklers, thick air fading for relief.
Water composes us & covers us, leaves us,
Opens & raises our arms in praise of cool.

& a garden hose sends the little ones
Screaming with delight, wipes the street
Of sidewalk chalk, meets lips of the shirtless
& tank-topped, anoints the organic. The hose
Washes day away. Mother holds the ground
Close, listens for its heartbeat, the lifeblood

Washed from her cheek by hose water
That will seep & flow its way to a drain,
Some pipeline labyrinth carrying witness
Out to sea, diluting vibrancy. Call it a cover-up,
Casting the distance between memory
& re-membering. One repeats its fading

Fragments. The other ordains wholeness. This,
Our daunting sail forward through stillness
& storm, hot, rising from the tide, ever rising.

Threnody: Your Boom & Treble Silence

for Jake Adam York

As your broadcast reaches through the void
Now beyond the Milky Way—that hulking band
Of loud light in silence—streams of teargas in Missouri
Fire the memory of your eyes, rubber bullets
Bruise the August dusk. The night is most honest
To these bodies, their voices martyred. Canisters hiss,
Muzzles crack the air. Your absence is the crackle
Of vinyl between tracks, the final spins of a record.

•

From the lectern you transmit & receive the word
Of this warfare world. You, a transistor for history,
For scratches & cracks in the vinyl. You, calm
First mate of a way downriver, to the gulf's mouth—
Open water. Your elegy of mellow seas & a low radio.
Your steady echo, its pulsing transmission enlisting
Listeners. *Listen!* your quiet pauses blare. *Listen
For the voices, the fading pulse, the growing rift.*

•

Nearly two years, twenty, some centuries down
The line, the human strings your fingers fluttered
Hum the wood of memory a little longer. Poplars
Bear the marks of knives, ropes, the shouts of mobs
& lovers. You sound the rings of a poplar's age,
Token that history grows wide in us, that our mouths
Drink language of the past, that the barbs are ever sharp
In the gut. Hollow spin of your ended record, calm sea
In your aftermath, you call in silence booming, ellipsized—
The bleeding throat, tongue's last epileptic flutter—

Whiteness As Hyperbolic Bass Line

You'd think you'd hear it—
    Overblown, blowing up
        Your mind, the dial over-

           Turned, woofer flowing
Flowing a fat vibrating tongue-
    Hum. You'd hear it if you thought
        It could save you. You'll do anything

        For a bit of salvation, any
Damn thing to be wrapped in blue
    Neon, in a smokebox basement
        With a quintet of angels hammering
           Out chords & a few squeaky notes.

    Forget them pearly whatchamacallits.

You're here for instant rapture. Here to melt
    In the span of a tune—ice slipping
        Into brown liquor, distilled comfort
           Into your daylong stupor. You'll hear it

Blowing up your chest after a few more,
    When the ceiling lowers its ninth cloud.
        Leaning back on rickety legs, you'd think
        You'd hear salvation

Laying you low, running its tongue
    Through your veins. You'd think
        You were being thrummed
        Out of this world or farther into it.

    But what's the difference, really?

        In some kind of heaven, we hear
        What we don't want to, here.

The Salt Craving

after Dizzy Gillespie & Charlie Parker

How you utter a word
      Changes its salt. *Salt peanuts*
         Whispered, hummed, signals
Elegy. A raspy squeal
      Turns them punch-

         Line, strolling into a bar.
I hear the earthy notes in them
      Roasting, hear them spread
         Across my tongue, naked
& gnashed to pieces, to butter. & that sting—

      Salt dissolves slick sidewalks,
         Seasons just about everything,
Bites & bites back after every bite
      Torturing the tongue. I scoop
         Another handful because I need the lash

Of sound's salt. I lash my mind
      With the ingenuity we have
         For salt & sound. Preserve
Flesh. Sterilize. Memorialize. Make the wound.
      Pack the wound. Don't you know

         Torture is a salted imagination? Didn't I
Horn you about punchlines? Didn't
      I line you up & suckerpunch you
         With my horn? *salt Peanuts!*
salt Peanuts! Don't you understand

      Every trumpeted tone is a grain of blue
         Salt squeezed out sideways, a grain
Of sound I'm dropping
      On the tongue, because you want
         Its sting that badly, over & again?

Litany of Hustle

Hustle the beat, double-time doubled.
Hustle from your second to your third job.
Hustle hard & hustle smart but hustle nonetheless.
Hustle, or else. Hustle tongue-poised to the neck line,
Hustle to the inner thigh, to the trap wrapped in silence.
Hallowed be thy hustle.
Hustle as in double work, double effort.
Hustle as in dupe the dope.
Hustle wit & smoke & midnight.
Hustle down a consequence, a banded wad.
Hustle in your comfort. Hustle from behind.
Hustle from the corner. Hustle up the mind.
Hustle as the bougainvillea hustles the trellis.
Hustle court-wise, yearlong, dusk to dawn to dusk to dawn & on.
Hustle up a high-rise, down & up again.
This is a hustle-off—rhythm of days, days, days, days, days, days, days, days.
Hustle the wind, the improvised explosive device, the drone, steel cuffs.
Hustle the drone of a migraine.
Hustle the kneed back & tensed shoulder.
Hustle the hustler & the hustled.
Hustle like the Big Bang boomerang.
Hustle into a hologram. Hustle hurdle, higher, higher, higher still.
Hustle savagely, scavenge scrappily & hardscrabble for the scrap
Pat on the back. Hustle for the loose ball, the jump ball
To the baseline & beyond. Hush about your hustle.
Bear your body on a gamble. Hustle in a rush.
Hustle Hercules's muscle to an arm-wrestle victory.
Hustle the river-flow. Hustle the space-time continuum.
Hustle Heraclitus himself. Hustle Socrates & society.
Hustle highbrow or high hat or high beams or high head.
Hustle the hardheads, the hardness, the head the head the head.
Hustle hyperactive. Hustle the Jack of Hearts hustling the two
To the ten, one after the other, hustling. Round up your hustle,
Corral your heartache, then ride those horses coast to coast
To coast to death. Then ride death. Break that pale stallion.

The Emperor of White Smoke

Let be be finale of seem.
    —Wallace Stevens

He seems elliptical, as in cigar
Rings bangling his wrists, as in the circular whip
Of his lips, his tongue meat like curds,
Words billowing smoky, dressing
His hamster-wheel logic limited to boys
In which he is the hamster soiling shredded newspaper
& the wheel making speedy, lightfooted love.
Every figment fancies himself the emperor of white smoke.

Struck & stroked, an ego is a deal
Wherein the handshake does not release, the sheet
Of his offenses trails, another body's weight & another. Once
Or twice the hands fall & rise, his face
Shifts, a cloud thinning. He is coming
Again to the land of the dumb,
Has packed all his certitude, his hazy ambition into a joke.
Every figment fantasies himself the white emperor of smoke.

Whiteness

This blizzard swarms as time

Swarms, stings, crowds us

Relentlessly, all deepfreeze & wind.

Flakes, weightless bone shards,

Attack from the flanks. From every sky

A blitzkrieg of little devils,

Their wily antics, their grave

Burrowing beyond skin & calcium

To what must be our ghost

Intangible in the marrow. This white,

Not the invisible freeze. Not

Sacrificial pilots. Neither the intangible

Undermining nor a coat of frozen

Throwing stars, melded ice locking

Us in place. What swarms & stings

Camouflages with blizzard. It works

From far off, commanding wind

& chill & fluid word;

It works from within

Like time, beneath the skin,

In every bone, ungraspable

In there.

•

History is over, you all, and everything's ahead at last.

—Toni Morrison, *Jazz*

Blood, not as in power but the echo of it, and the echo fading—

—Carl Phillips, "Ransom"

This Time, Fire

combustion

& you must remain in the fire
of your own burn hollers a prophet.
Whatever flame you cradle turns you
in its tumble, whip of lick, flash & vanish.

keeper

The time of the end is misconception.
Our clocks hinge
                    on a center point.
If deities rely on the circle
for message,
                    breaking geometry
in that time at the end
makes for their destruction.
Time as linear,
                    as liner, lint, links, limited,
as at-once leviathan. Maybe
time should make less sense.
For a time & times
                    & half a time, silence
burned in heaven for half an hour.

Qiblah

Five times a day, hum
smolders through me.

Five times each day
I tremble for blaze.

Toss me to the most high sound,
your skin's scorching phrase.

calamity

Admit me to the fire
like sugar cane's slashed stalks.
A second death & scorching
wind. Usher me—clean—

comparison

Persecution is worse than slaying.
Percussion
            or silence?

clock talk

Krishna ignites their audience:

*I am terrible
Time the destroyer of all
Beings in all worlds*

Time, the infinite flame—

Qiblah

Meet me, friction, source
of heat & renewal. Make me.

combustion II

Clothed with flesh or fabric or sun
or some sort of sin, you cannot escape
your fuel. Strike at the foe's head
with a bare foot. Live at the edge
of combustion & you're bound to be lit.

consumption

O fired word, be coolness
& peace, taste the doom of burning.
To bring heat you must consume
a thing unto char. Wrap yourself,
flame, around those too sparse to catch.

You shall abide, you shall abide.

captivity

Holding a note until your lungs
empty—
         Taking sound hostage—
Stoking the fire until all fuel is spent—
Glaring into the massless mass of light,
hot hues, endless—
         Listening—
to a string of cracks, consistent hiss—

eating through kindling—
                    No,
that is the sound of you, joints,
where the language of light takes you,
if you aren't careful—

Qiblah

Toss me to the most high sound, your scorching phrase.

concussive

Teach me to keep open my throat, hawk
the round body of the letter Q out of me.
I've never been good at shots, belting out
notes, remaining wide as a tunnel—
people & sound trekking in both heated directions.

calamity II

Usher me to the first trumpet's blast,
thunder shrieking through brush,

through me, clearing the field,
breath of the divine—basic obliteration.

cleanse

My tongue extinguishes
& blazes with equal measure.

Qiblah

Five times each day I tremble for blaze.

catch

Only a burnt child dreads the fire.
Only a burnt child dreads the fire.
Only a burnt child. Admit me
to the light where I may finally learn
dread. Hard to understand a desire like that—
this is how I might atone. How history
& the word will fasten my hands
around a post, as they have
for others forever, & toss a tongue
into the pine needles beneath. Only this will do.

quietude

I will not make long fire here.

characterized

In the Qu'ran, Allah is not described
as all-seeing, as I was told
those many months of Sundays. Instead,
the deity hears all. When I light the stove
It hears gas ignite. When I flash
a muzzle, *They* hear every shot.
When I snuff my mind, *You* hear the smoke.

Qiblah

Five times a day, hum smolders through me.

confession

Distracted by my own light,
                      I forgot to burn.

What Is Given, What Is Done

●

Inheritance is a rifle
We accept with little
Consideration. With

Nostalgia, reverence
For the life had, we
Will keep the past

Thriving. We will
Care for the barrel,
Brush the bolt & firing

Pin, keep the stock's
Memory of holding.
Every surface we deem

Holy; every flaw we
Make shine. We man
The safety, the trigger,

& climb into the chamber.
You make my aerodynamics
Unforgettable, ancestors,

Shape me sharp, file me
& tip me with mercury.
O, what tradition bores—

•

If I become a hand palm

Flat & face-up   If I kneel

At the feet of the wounded

Mangled defiled generations

If I kiss the earth-bound

Bodies open my mouth

For the spirits unending   If

I exalt the colorful spectrum

Of woven threads fierce

Muscle of every body

Tightening in thrall

& jubilation   If we smelt

The metal repurpose wood

Into gift   If we wrap danced

Legs & blend our sweat breathe

Breath not our body's   If we

Melt our lips with another's song—

If Smoke Could Sing

history would be more reliable

every bite of meat would tell you a story

maybe we'd be better listeners

we would call them song-bombs

or song-grenades hurled into a crowd

how loud would the sound rise

we would smell music

all the burning buildings & crematoriums

what more might become ash

perhaps leaving the beloved would be less of a shock

snuff me now—

How to Flip the Beat

When glass or glass water flips the skyline,
Lines against the sky, sky against the lines;
When color lines run parallel, the definition
Of never touching; when cityscapes get flipped
By nightsticks & Maglites; when lights
Magnify the bruise; when suburban grids
Sprawl; when sprawl is a face-down position,
Fingers itching to escape; when city blocks bruise
Orange with street lamp; when engine idle
Breathes the metronome for your morning;
When the beat keeper keeps the beats from you
It beats keeping up with bruises; when blue

Flashes stutter red, cold-hot on cinderblock;
When your block smolders with the cinders
Of slugs, souls flung from their copper
Casings; when hammers drive combustion;
When hammers drive the rail tie, when white
Is a clean sheet, a pasty face, a mean beat;
When fear rattles off its mating call; when
You think you hear violence; when honesty
Loses its fierce stride; when glass buildings
Look back at you, the mirror of a city's
State of mind; when concrete makes love
To busted windows; when orange light dyes

The window shards; when windows
& eyes die; when wardrobes turn orange;
When it's easier to wear dread
On your face; when dread is a teardrop
Inked near your eye; when bruises
Remind you of your skin or the dark
Of your lover's eye; when bar bells drop

Like hammers in the yard, in the garage;
When bells mean *funeral*; when shots
Wake you from a dream of the first time
You feel the beat of a belly, when you fall
Into the beat's sweet thump, thump-thump?

If *Riot* Means Destruction

Without the moon we find   our lightness   whiteness

Washed out brightness   coming down on us   a baton of

Unconsciousness   unconscienceness   the breakage we

Didn't know we could bring   riot is not reaction   it is

Burning down from within   how we burn an other's body

Down quietly   over time   keep the ember humming

Blowing   blowing   blow   until the tongue flares

Sizzled & singeing   riot is the mind of whiteness

Looting stores propped in the chest   robbing water &

Bread to break down   the head & will of an other   the

Riot begins with silence   with an attack   a drone strike

A sniper some mile off   every voice in the street   fist   cry

Every face in the eye   of a camera is not   a riot

Not a threat   a force to stop traffic   bring on the red lights

Shut down the headlights   eager to blind   bring down

The sky   the moon   bring down   bring down

Uprising

1992 & 20 miles south bloom spring plumes
Of car-smoke, smoke-bombs, boom the sound clouds
Of municipal bullet mobs. Bashed glass rings—a city fault-line
Faltering. White noise & those whom it silences
Clashing, generations clanging. How high does the city's rupture rise?
How far does it ripple? Over miles, years. I didn't have the math yet.
Still learning basic addition, how to grow my candy stash.
My mind that raw doesn't draw conclusions
From black trails rising or news anchors' uncanny castings—
Even reports of death come grinning.
I don't add street names to parks; neighborhoods don't add up
To more than friends' houses.
Deductions come later, much later,
With economic calculus: the freeway is tolled,
Measured in lives & lineage. It is denial
Compounded, exponential, reflexive. L.A. landslides
Itself, buries itself, the transitive properties of public housing
& gated communities. The wide lane crams
With black-geared figures, anointed by silver-shield shimmer
& single-syllable grunts. My wide lane brims silence—
                                        Dad arrives home, news looping
With the steam of spaghetti. Another any-day,
Voices not exactly soundless, but asking *How
Was work? Was the drive OK?* I did not yet have the drive
To ask about the televised faces I'm certain I read.
Calculate: denial equals uprising, no matter what you add.
Nightstick plus shirtless is greater than busted rib
& bluing psyche. & if silence equals history,
& history hitches itself to me, then I become a more silent me.
I rise in silence. No voice rises
On my subtle street. None figure I could come up
Locked behind a body-shaped shield,
Flashing the invisible badge pinned on me
By some legacy. Silence rises. Turn up the TV, it's seven o'clock.
That equals *Jeopardy!* or *Star Trek: The Next Generation.*

Disturbance

It wakes me
In the chest
In the smallest hours

The neighbor needs
His blaring-music lovin
His car-cocoon of sound

& it wakes me
Like the bathroom door creak
Like a forgotten

I've remembered like lightning
In the poem I've forgotten
Like my wife adjusting

Her calmest face of blue
Finding better comfort
Her fingers unfurling

Near my thigh the rumble
Wakes me as it is meant to
Always stirring the blood

The brain the steady current
Of sleep or thinking the subwoofer
Makes a pace & interrupts

As it was meant to

Bass Tone Ode

Dear heavy note, dear key of gloom, you loom
     Low in my gut, a slow bloom, bottom feeder
Of longing. You, the final sound of water

     Swallowing the body. You, the far end of a piano
Keeping time for the funeral. You, the kiss
     I wake to every day. In your steady hum, the river

Hollows like a bone in the earth, loses its meat,
     Thins because that's how sorrow works. Dear stone
Striking an empty oil drum, dear breast-beating

     Fist, this hole in the mist of a winter dark morning.
Your drone, a thread, rising & sinking its long
     Frequency, why the foghorn groans so shallow

Its impossible exhale. If I listen long enough,
     If I lay down my cloth, perhaps, after the song,
Its many years, you will slide through, I will learn

     Your pulse & pass it forward, loud.

Transubstantiation

Where light bruises the air
Discreetly, time turns to smoke. Walk
Through & it dominates.
                        Passing a mirror
I catch the curve of an ear, a foreign
Gait, how the right shoulder dips more deeply
Than the left. I turn my hand in the air
& the vein that writhes is not mine. I know,
Somehow, it is that of a man I've seen
Only in photos.
                        In one he stands nearby
My mother. I lean against his left leg
Just grown enough to wobble. Wherever
We stand, the light is remnant—low glow
Of a hushed wick.
                        & there, his face is not his,
Nor his gut. He has become his great-
Grandfather, whose hand commands the over-
Seer. Smoke trails litter the valley there,
Fields purple with ground fog, ripen with blood.
& here my blood loops, smoke in that light.

Another Sip

In from the shack where she hung tobacco thick,
In from the field where she smothered herself

With tomato hearts, in from the yard where she scattered
Her sister's untended clothes, at the table

Her father warned, *You'll turn black*
If you drink coffee too young, little one.

His knuckle-crowned hand, his single-tined tongue,
Both driven hard by a rusting mind,

Lodged sharper & farther than sticker bush thorns in my mother.
Humans invented faith

For the child's mind. Believe in the switch
For you must retrieve it. Smother yourself

With prayer & penance. Trust in wrath.
When a child prays, they break

Open for the whims of elders. They are saved
By a palm pat on the head. A child is wildest

Yet most pious. Threaten the backhand,
Threaten withholding, threaten with a lie.

We are threatened & then do the threatening,
Busted & cobbled at the edges.

A spirit conducts these rooms & corridors,
Our moving through them. Spirit of the many,

Spirit relentless. Tell me another story,
Mother, give me more past to heave & burn.

Night Interrogates the Light Bulb

I blare my 40 watts up into the darkening
Vast warehouse of evening. A god

Lords over me, wide, unwieldy,
Firing questions from all the infinite

Points of light shoving their way
Into the fray. My bald face, pale

& emitting, weakens. *What made you*
Think to shine so hard? I flicker for once.

Why do you swivel toward the many
Infinitesimals? I learn the lifeblood

Of second-guessing. *You, too, are a speck,*
One among the throngs. All you need

Is a pinprick of doubt. Never imagined
Quieting the light could mean as much as

Or more than illumination. I am still here, lit,
Liminal, straddling my past of blinding

& my now—comfort disrupted
For a buzzless moment in a field

Of questions, everything thriving in night,
Darkness's broad & graceful arm

Around my shoulder.

Exodus, Still

after & for Eduardo C. Corral

I started making my way out of the desert

At 25, without knowing

                The desert would end.

My hands, by then, had become pincers.

                    My tongue, a stinger.

Night joined me like a friend. After dusk

We tore up the place. I fed.

                Someone died every night.

The day's buzzing heat erased mountains

& cactus towers

            All reappearing after dark.

Still, I scrape through these flats,

                Steer to a star,

A cluster or constellation shaped like a hand,

A whole body

           I was meant to have

& use as a well,

        Ferry handfuls from a cool depth

To prey.

        That body, meant to find predators,

Reveal the gnaw-marks on their own hinds,

An accidental puncture of the spine.

                Toward that star

& by night

        I scrounge through sagebrush

Until first light.

        When I reach the edge of the desert

Where stars lie in horizon's dust,

            I, too, will lie down.

Plea

Swing low swing low sweet sweet chariot.
Nothing but a plain black boy.
　　　—Gwendolyn Brooks

Swing slick your silver scythe. Swing slow, decisive, your thick hammer.
Low swung & lying low, you drive boys down with your clicked hammer.

Swing by. We'll sling sighs the size of freighters loaded down & sluggish, horns'
Low tone growing enlarged hearts. Then, to the taut muscles, a blue-sick hammer.

Sweet flow, stealth mode, blows the blood in vain. These flow, the little rivers,
Sweet & deep. Until, at fourteen or forty-nine, a dam drops—the final tick hammers.

Chariot wheeling free in fury. I fly, its charioteer, into the ravine of vengeance.
Nothing will escape my blade, not even me. & the sea collapses its reddening hammer.

But, *a jury*. But, *peers*. (Who, really, thinks of human beings with that word?) But, *a judge*,
Plain & pious to a law. If we want justice, we have to trust those quick hammers—*hmmm*—

Black robe. Black leather case. Briefs redacted black. Brief, the verdict; brief, the sentence.
Boy, it's final. Its gavel-smack, spinal. It is wooden & revered: the almighty, slick hammer.

●

I swing wild, plow the mirror's boy, swing low blows for sweet & unsweet spots. I chariot
Nothing innocent, & I feed you a plain, blacked out body—Wesley, licked & hammered.

Kneebone in the Wilderness

This continent that brings me to my knees
  Knows a wildness, a bone-raking
Meanstreak. This pale beach I've landed,
  This continent in me plants me
Firmly in its hands. Brought by the vessel
  Historia, I drag ashore my anchor iron.

    Kneebone bend to save my soul.

Bend to this foreign sun. Kneel for mercy
  That will not come. Learn dirtied blood & salt
In soil. Become a stone of this earth.
  I bring rhythm, my worship, harness the stomp
& clap of rising embers. I bring beating
  To its knees. With my beat kneeling down
I am free from its beating. I am free of this
  Hard-dying continent in me.

    Kneebone bend to save my soul.

& when my legs are taken at the knee,
  Hands from the wrist, tongue from my low
Laid throat, I will bend what whisper
  Of me remains, begging the penitent continent
To allow me some spit of land, begging pardon
  With praise & bone on whatever knee I can improvise.

Notes

The Ralph Ellison epigraph is the final sentence of *Invisible Man* without the final two words, "for you."

The James Baldwin epigraph originally appeared in his August 1965 *Ebony* essay, "The White Man's Guilt," which was later slightly revised & anthologized with a different title: "Unnameable Objects, Unspeakable Crimes."

"Request Aubade" is dedicated to Prince.

"The Invention of Clock Theory" borrows language from "The Message," by Grandmaster Flash & the Furious Five. Clock theory, otherwise known as punch phrasing, is a mixing technique often credited to Grandmaster Flash.

"Rum & Raspberries" references data reported in an article for *The Guardian*, 20 April 2009.

"I Pledge" is after Roger Reeves's poem "Pledge."

"Sinnerman" is after Nina Simone's rendition of the spiritual.

"Oyster Elegy" is for Michael Wiegers, Joseph Bednarik, & George Knotek.

"SAMO© Blues" is dedicated to Jean-Michel Basquiat.

"Baptism" is dedicated to Michael Brown, his mother, & you.

"Threnody: Your Boom & Treble Silence" ends with lines from Jake Adam York's poem, "Sensitivity."

The title "Whiteness As Hyperbolic Bass Line" borrows language from Yusef Komunyakaa's poem "Copacetic Mingus."

"The Salt Craving" improvises with the bebop tune "Salt Peanuts," composed by Dizzy Gillespie & Kenny Clarke in 1942, & performed most famously by Dizzy Gillespie, Charlie Parker, Al Haig, Curley Russell, & Sidney Catlett on 11 May 1945.

"The Emperor of White Smoke" takes liberties with the end words & title of Wallace Stevens's poem "The Emperor of Ice-Cream."

"This Time, Fire" borrows language from James Baldwin, the Qu'ran, the Bhagavad Gita, as well as Hebrew & Christian scripture. The Martin Luther King, Jr., epigraph is from his "Letter from Birmingham Jail."

"Uprising"—The Los Angeles Uprising followed the acquittal of police officers responsible for severely beating Rodney King. Between 29 April and 4 May 1992, 55 people were killed, more than 2,000 people were injured, & more than 11,000 people were arrested.

"Plea" hybridizes a ghazal with a golden shovel—a golden ghazal.

"Kneebone in the Wilderness" is after the ring shout "Kneebone Bend," & is dedicated to Afaa Michael Weaver.

After receiving an M.F.A. from Emerson College, Wesley Rothman taught writing & cultural literatures in Boston. His poems & criticism have appeared in *Boston Review, Callaloo, Gulf Coast, Harvard Review, New England Review, Prairie Schooner, Publishers Weekly, Southern Humanities Review,* & *The Golden Shovel Anthology,* among other venues. A Teaching Artist for the National Gallery of Art & recipient of a Vermont Studio Center Fellowship, he lives in Washington, D.C.

The New Issues Poetry Prize

Courtney Kampa, *Our Lady of Not Asking Why*
2016 Judge: Mary Szybist

Sawnie Morris, *Her Infinite*
2015 Judge: Major Jackson

Abdul Ali, *Trouble Sleeping*
2014 Judge: Fanny Howe

Kerrin McCadden, *Landscape with Plywood Silhouettes*
2013 Judge: David St. John

Marni Ludgwig, *Pinwheel*
2012 Judge: Jean Valentine

Andrew Allport, *the body | of space | in the shape of the human*
2011 Judge: David Wojahn

Jeff Hoffman, *Journal of American Foreign Policy*
2010 Judge: Linda Gregerson

Judy Halebsky, *Sky=Empty*
2009 Judge: Marvin Bell

Justin Marks, *A Million in Prizes*
2008 Judge: Carl Phillips

Sandra Beasley, *Theories of Falling*
2007 Judge: Marie Howe

Jason Bredle, *Standing in Line for the Beast*
2006 Judge: Barbara Hamby

Katie Peterson, *This One Tree*
2005 Judge: William Olsen

Kevin Boyle, *A Home for Wayward Girls*
2004 Judge: Rodney Jones

Matthew Thorburn, *Subject to Change*
2003 Judge: Brenda Hillman

Paul Guest, *The Resurrection of the Body and the Ruin of the World*
2002 Judge: Campbell McGrath

Sarah Mangold, *Household Mechanics*
2001 Judge: C.D. Wright

Elizabeth Powell, *The Republic of Self*
2000 Judge: C.K. Williams

Joy Manesiotis, *They Sing to Her Bones*
1999 Judge: Marianne Boruch

Malena Mörling, *Ocean Avenue*
1998 Judge: Philip Levine

Marsha de la O, *Black Hope*
1997 Judge: Chase Twichell